Natalia Maguire

# GREAT
## to be
## a DAD

Illustrated by
Anastasia Zababashkina

ISBN: 978-3-9821428-6-9

For more information please contact
Natalia Magvayr
Maguire Books
Parkstrasse 8, 22605 Hamburg, Germany

Visit our website at: www.maguirebooks.com

First printed and bound in the USA.

To the coolest Dads - past, present and future...

When I'm the Daddy of the house
And more than six feet tall,
My kids will have the coolest time
'Cos I'll decide it all.

I'll make the rules, and nobody
Can tell me what to do.
I'll stay at home and tell the kids

THEre's no more
school for you!

We'll get up late, at half past ten,
A whole day's play ahead -
No need to wash or brush our teeth,
No need to make the bed.

At breakfast time, no healthy food,
No tea with wholemeal bread,
Just pancakes with some chocolate sauce
And lemonade instead.

No need to stay in if there's rain -
We're off to play outdoors.
And rain clothes we will never need
Not even when it pours.

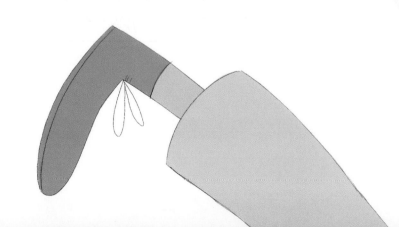

It's lunch time now and time to try
Exciting new cuisine,
Like burgers in a wine gum sauce
With lashings of whipped cream.

Oh, what a mess we've gone and made
Those dishes, such a pile!
But when my kids can help me clean
It only takes a while.

Instead of school I'll give my kids
My laptop and my phone.
They'll be the greatest gamers that
The world has ever known.

Enough of study, now it's time
For us to have some fun.
The water park would then be next
And when at last we're done,

We'll hurry home and order in
A dinner fit for kings.
With pizza, pasta, and a ton
Of spicy chicken wings.

It's getting late, but do we care?
No work or school, you see.
Oh, I can't wait till I'm the Dad.
How great it all will be!

But wait a minute, what's that noise?
No dreaming anymore!
'Cos now's the best time of the day

My daddy's at the door!

And so our hero liked to dream
Of when he'd be the dad,
But what do you think? Tell me, please
The thoughts that you have had.

Printed in Poland
by Amazon Fulfillment
Poland Sp. z o.o., Wrocław